Environmental
AMERICA

Environmental
AMERICA

The Southwestern States

by
D.J. Herda

The Millbrook Press
Brookfield, CT
The American Scene

Cover photographs (clockwise from top) courtesy of
D. J. Herda; U.S. Forest Service; D. J. Herda (2)

Photographs courtesy of
Wisconsin Dept. of Natural Resources: 16, 27, 50; D. J. Herda: 6, 9, 10, 13, 30, 34, 40, 54;
Tom Stack & Associates: 15, 21, 24; Environmental Protection Agency: 33, 37; Mammal
Slide Library, C. E. Chehebar: 44

Designed by Moonlit Ink, Madison, WI 53705
Illustrations by Renee Graef

Cataloging-in-Publication Data
Herda, D. J.
Environmental America: The Southwestern States.
Brookfield, CT, The Millbrook Press. 1991.
64 p.; col. ill.; (The American Scene)
Includes bibliographical references and index.
Summary: The impact of humankind and society on the environment, with special
emphasis on the Southwestern region.
ISBN 1-878841-11-4   639.9 HER

1. Southwest states—environmental impacts—juvenile literature. 2. Conservation of
natural resources. 3. Pollution. [1. Environmental America: The Southwestern States]
I Title. II. Series.

C O N T E N T S

INTRODUCTION

Imagine yourself traveling through the American Southwest. As you pass through California, Nevada, Utah, Colorado, Arizona, New Mexico, and the Pacific island state of Hawaii, you see strangely beautiful plants, animals, and geologic formations. You experience blazing hot temperatures and low humidities, mile after mile of windswept sands and blinding sun. You find very little water in the deserts of California, Nevada, Arizona, and New Mexico. Some receive less than 5 inches of rain a year!

When nighttime comes, desert temperatures drop sharply. Only those plants and animals that have adapted to life under these unusually harsh conditions can survive.

But the desert, while making up a major part of the Southwest, is only one component of the region's environment. The area also boasts large stretches of open prairie lands broken by several strings of high mountain ranges laced with aspen, scrub oak, and evergreen trees. Mountain temperatures are much more moderate than those in the desert, and the plants and animals that live here are different.

Hawaii, too, has mountains, although its climate is more temperate than that of the other southwestern states. Lush foliage and colorful flowers carpet Hawaii's valleys, and exotic creatures perfectly adapted to island living inhabit the chain of eight islands constituting the state.

(opposite page)
The southwestern United States boasts geologic formations unlike anywhere else in the world.

THE BEGINNINGS OF LIFE

Although the actual beginnings of life on Earth are unclear, fossils show what anthropologist Loren Eiseley once called "the long war of life against its inhospitable environment."

Early in Earth's history, the relentless rays of the sun bombarded the planet, scorching its sands and searing its barren rock. The simple atmosphere contained only a few basic gases and water vapor. There was little or no oxygen.

Eventually, the Earth's physical forces—sunlight, water, and wind—interacted to produce an environment capable of supporting the growth of simple, one-celled plant organisms. These plants drew carbon from existing carbon dioxide gas and used the energy of the sun to create the basic sugars, or carbohydrates, necessary for life. As the plants flourished, they gave off oxygen. The oxygen generated by the plants was held near the surface of the planet by Earth's gravitational pull and eventually formed an atmosphere suitable for more advanced forms of life.

EARTH'S CHANGING BIOSPHERE

During the millions of years in which life has evolved on Earth, the biosphere—that part of the planet capable of supporting life—has undergone many changes. Mountains have risen and eroded away, worn back down to sand and soil by natural causes. Great sheets of ice have come and gone. Giant tree ferns, dinosaurs, and other plants and animals have lived, died, and vanished from the Earth.

Earth's living biosphere has been growing, expanding, shrinking, and changing since the beginning of life. How and when it will stop—if ever—is anyone's guess. Keeping it healthy is everyone's job.

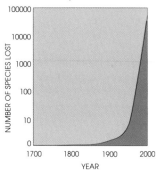

Estimated Annual Rate of Species Loss, 1700-2000

NUMBER OF SPECIES LOST

100000
10000
1000
100
10
0

1700   1800   1900   2000

YEAR

Source: Based on estimates in Norman Myers (Ed., Gaia: An Atlas of Planet Management (Garden City, NY: Anchor Books, 1984), p. 155

(opposite page)
Prickly pear cactus blossoms burst into color in early spring.

CHAPTER ONE

THE WEB OF LIFE

Life in the Southwest exists wherever it can gain a foothold. Gnarled Rocky Mountain oaks and stately pinyon pines sprout from sheer cliff walls. Desert shrimp hatch in temporary puddles where they mature, breed, and later die as the puddles dry up. White pocket mice and pale desert lizards skip across scorching desert sands. Algae grow in the scalding hot waters of natural springs.

As many as 40 million plant, animal, and insect species inhabit the Earth, each of which has conditions beyond which it cannot survive. As many as 20 percent of these species, according to *The Global 2000 Report to the President*, could disappear by the year 2000. That's nearly 8 million species! As many as a thousand species are currently becoming extinct each and every year—a rate of nearly three a day. Extinction of these species on such a large scale is unprecedented in human history.

OUR LIVING ECOSYSTEM

Over the years, Earth's plants and animals have gradually evolved as part of living systems, called ecosystems, in which all life is interrelated. The largest ecosystems, called biomes, consist of grasslands, tropical rain forests, deciduous forests, coniferous forests, tundras, coastal wetlands, and deserts. Each biome varies greatly in climate and physical makeup.

Throughout the Southwest, caves, rock faces, and even cakes of salt are capable of supporting life. Yet the story of environmental America in the Southwest is as much a story of death as of life. It's a story of abuse and greed, of thoughtless-

(opposite page)
Desert lizards warm themselves in the hot Arizona sun.

ness and negligence. It's the story of a magnificent, fragile land brutalized by humankind.

PRAIRIE LANDS UNDER SIEGE

The prairie lands of the Southwest, with their millions of acres of open pastures, once held the promise of new wealth for ranchers who could herd the greatest number of cattle across them. By the 1860s, railroads, refrigerator cars, and steamships had opened new markets for southwestern beef, and cattlemen and sheepherders grazed their stock in ever-increasing numbers. Eventually, these numbers proved too large for the dry, fragile lands to support. In their rush to make fortunes, ranchers destroyed the very lands on which they relied for their livelihoods.

As the livestock began overgrazing the lands, the grass grew thin and weak. Normal periods of drought turned rich fields of green into barren deserts. Land that had once supported a hundred steers soon could support only fifty, then fewer.

Winds sweeping across the open range kicked up the exposed soil and carried it far away. More winds came and more soil disappeared. Then heavy rains washed much of the remaining soil away. As the rich, fertile topsoil disappeared, weeds such as thistle and poisonous Klamath spread over huge areas.

Still the homesteaders and settlers moved into the area, each one hoping to tame the land and make a living from the range. They tilled up the remaining sod in order to plant crops of wheat and hay. In the process, still more native grass was lost, and more soil vanished in the wind.

In less than half a century, humankind in its ignorance had turned rich, fertile land that had lived in harmony with nature for millions of years into barren wasteland. Nearly all that remained were sprawling stands of sagebrush, tumbleweed, and other useless shrubs.

Even the animals suffered. As the rangelands disappeared, so did thousands of species of insects, birds, reptiles, and mammals that had once called them home. Farmers and ranchers poisoned and shot coyotes on sight. Populations of

gophers and other burrowing animals, no longer held in check by their natural predators, exploded. Soon, millions of burrowing animals crisscrossed the countryside, digging up what remained of the original sod and adding to the problem of erosion.

Grazing cattle soon turn fragile southwestern lands into wind-blown deserts.

THE WEB IS BROKEN

The steadily eroding soil kept buffalo and other hardy prairie grasses from reseeding, leading to more erosion. Eroding soil washed into lakes, streams, and rivers, clogging them with silt and killing off aquatic life.

Not even the giant saguaro cactus, towering some 30 feet above the desert floor and weighing as much as 3 tons, was

spared. The saguaro, which sends out a large network of shallow roots that quickly absorb what little moisture falls from the sky, provides a home for gila woodpeckers. The birds lay their eggs in holes tapped in the side of the cactus. Once the holes are abandoned, purple martins and elf owls quickly claim them for their own.

Today, the saguaro are disappearing. People pouring out of nearby cities and towns, seeking an escape from the congestion, smog, and stress of daily life, are slowly taking over the land on which they grew.

DESERT SOIL DESTRUCTION

Thousands of recreational vehicles cross deserts such as the Chihuahuan of Texas, New Mexico, and Arizona; the Painted of northern Arizona; the Sonoran of southwestern Arizona and southeastern California; and Death Valley of eastern California and southwestern Nevada. Their wheels compact the soil so that scarce rains can no longer be absorbed and used by desert cactuses and other plants. The plants receive heavy damage as their roots are battered and cut. Many of them die from dehydration, or lack of water.

Desert birds lose their natural nesting sites. Exploding insect populations, no longer held in check by the birds, attack hay and croplands and destroy valuable resources. Anxious farmers spray their fields with pesticides to kill the insects. Some pesticides are consumed by grazing cattle and enter our food chain. Others wash into nearby rivers and streams. Unless something is done soon to stop the damage to our environment, we may find ourselves living in a world with fewer natural biomes, less food to eat, and less clean water to drink.

How much of our nation's environmental web still remains intact? Perhaps far less than we realize. Certainly far less than we'd like to think.

(opposite page)
Saguaro cactus tower high above the Southwest's desert floors.

THE LAND WE WALK

Many people think of the Southwest as a dry, lifeless expanse of hot, windswept sands. In reality, it contains numerous biomes teeming with life. For centuries, Hopi, Papago, and other Native American tribes have grown a wide variety of crops in the desert, most without any irrigation. Such plants as desert-adapted corn, beans, potatoes, peppers, melons, and squash, as well as panic grass, amaranth, and devil's claw, have long been staples in the diets of these tribes.[1]

Wildlife, too, is diverse in the desert, from the wild burros used by early prospectors to native bighorn sheep, coyotes, kit foxes, elf owls, desert tortoises, kangaroo rats, iguanas and other lizards, cactus wrens, and black-throated sparrows.[2]

How can animals live in the desert? How can plants grow in dry desert soils? The answer lies at the very base of the food chain with the creation of soil.

THE BIRTH OF THE LAND

Soil begins life as rock. The rock is slowly weathered, or broken into smaller particles, by the forces of water, wind, and sun and by the freezing-and-thawing cycles common at higher elevations.

The roots of living plants also help break large rocks into smaller ones and eventually into soil. This is especially true in fringe areas where the southwestern desert grudgingly gives way to the grasslands. There, lichens and mosses often attach themselves to bare rock. They soak up and hold water from rain and work their rootlike parts down into tiny crevices, opening up hairline cracks and splitting the rocks into smaller

(opposite page)
The rugged foothills and mountains of the Southwest jut up out of the desert.

segments. The weak acids produced by the plants help break
the rocks down chemically.

Dead plants—from cactuses in the desert to the blades of
grass on the prairie—also play a role in the creation of soil.
When a plant dies, it begins to decay. Eventually, lichens and
mosses begin feeding on it. On the ground beneath the plant,
various insects, worms, bacteria, and fungi help speed the process of decomposition. This breaks the plant down into more
basic elements.

Eventually, the plant is gone. In its place is a layer of black,
spongy humus created from wood, leaves, and other decaying
plant matter. Below that layer is a vein of brown
topsoil—sandy-textured rock particles broken down through
weathering. It's in this shallow layer of topsoil and humus
that new plants begin their life.

Various animals also play a part in the creation of soil. Small
tunneling animals create burrows that allow air and water to
work their way underground and mix with the soil. In doing
so, the animals eat young, tender plant roots. The animals'
solid wastes add more nutrients to the soil, resulting in fertile
growing conditions for plants.

As the small animals die, their bodies begin to decay,
adding more nutrients to the humus. The result: more humus,
more nutrients, more growing plants, more tunneling animals,
and so on. Since the beginning of life on Earth, this slowly
evolving process of soil making has helped change the barren
surface of the Southwest into a rich environment for living
organisms.

THE FOOD CHAIN

As important as soil is to the ecology of the Southwest, so too
plants are critical to the food chain—the vital chain of living
creatures that traces its main food source back to plants. A
typical southwestern food chain may start with a single blade
of grass. A mouse feeds on the grass; a hawk feeds on the
mouse; a fox feeds on the hawk; a mountain lion feeds on the
fox. If any one element in the food chain were to
disappear—the mouse or the hawk, for example—the balance
of nature would be upset, possibly with disastrous results.

Green plants are the base for life's food chain because they have the ability to make their own food from inorganic, or nonliving, materials. Except for this remarkable ability, every living thing on Earth, including human beings, would die.

LIVING FACTORIES

Green plants use their roots to absorb water and dissolved minerals from the soil. This solution of water and minerals is piped through the plants' veins, much the way blood travels through human veins, until it reaches the plants' leaves. There it combines with carbon dioxide, which plants take in through tiny openings, called stomata, on the underside of their leaves.

When sunlight strikes the leaves of a plant, millions of tiny packets of a green material called chlorophyll absorb the light energy and use it to change the solution into glucose, a type of sugar. The glucose acts as food for the plants, helping them to grow. In the process, excess oxygen is given off—the very same oxygen that all animals (including human beings) need to sustain life![3] This process of food making in plants is called photosynthesis. In turn, animals, which take in oxygen and give off carbon dioxide, help green plants to continue to manufacture food and produce even more oxygen.

THE ENCROACHING DESERT

Throughout the Southwest, especially in the fringe desert and grassland biomes, humankind has thoughtlessly upset the delicate balance of nature by moving onto the land, clearing forests, and plowing up hundreds of thousands of acres of grasslands. One of the results of this process is called desertification.

Desertification is the changing of productive lands into wastelands. It's happening in Colorado, where pasturelands have been invaded by mesquite, a worthless shrub that robs the soil of valuable nutrients and prevents grasses from growing. It's happening in Utah, where the land is succumbing to sagebrush. It's happening in New Mexico, Arizona, and southern California—throughout the Southwest, in fact, as well as in arid biomes around the world.

Overgrazing, unwise agricultural practices leading to erosion, unsound mining techniques, and careless recreational
use of our lands all play a major role in the problem. Slowly
but surely we're turning the globe into a scorching, barren
desert! In fact, the United Nations' Environmental Program
estimates that as many as 15 million acres of land worldwide
are turning into desert each year. Areas of low rainfall; long,
dry seasons; recurrent droughts; and sparse vegetation are
most susceptible—areas like those of the American Southwest![4]

Turning back the tides of desertification is neither easy nor
inexpensive. Preventing further desertification through governmental programs that restrict land use may be the world's
only hope. Until then, we're likely to see an ever-increasing
rate of desertification throughout the American Southwest
and much of the rest of the world—and with it, decreasing
food production and increasing deaths from starvation.

OUR ERODING SOIL

The destruction of one species in nature often leads to the
destruction of others. Yet humankind continues to upset the
balance of nature, often in a never-ending search for more
land to cultivate. In the process, soil that has taken thousands
of years to create disappears practically overnight.

Despite expenditures of more than $15 billion on soil con-
servation since the mid-1930s, topsoil losses in the United
States are up 25 percent. By 1981, the country was losing 4 billion tons of soil a year—enough to fill a train of freight cars
long enough to circle the globe 24 times!

The U.S. Department of Agriculture estimates today that
more than one third of all U.S. cropland is seriously affected
by some form of erosion. Much of that land may soon have to
be retired from agricultural use.

But the Southwest's environmental problems are hardly
confined to erosion. Cattle destined for market create tremen-
dous waste-disposal problems. Pesticides applied to farmers'
fields kill more than the organisms they were meant to
destroy. Rainwater washes polluting chemicals into rivers,
lakes, streams, and oceans. Irrigation raises the salt content of
topsoil until it's toxic both to plants and animals.

THE ENERGY DILEMMA

The energy industry, too, is a major polluter of the Southwest. Every burning light bulb, glowing television set, tumbling washing machine; every automobile, garage door opener, and elevator—everything, in fact, that runs on one form of power or another generates pollution.

Offshore oil rigs provide invaluable energy at a high risk to the environment.

Some of the world's most common fuels—coal, oil, and natural gas, called fossil fuels—were created over millions of years by the natural decomposition of plants and animals covered by layers of humus, silt, and other debris. Fossil fuels are used by most power plants to produce electricity for residential and commercial use. They are also the main source for fuels used to power cars, trucks, and other internal-combustion vehicles.

In order to extract coal from southwestern lands, huge amounts of topsoil are peeled back, exposing the land to both erosion and pollution. Strip-mining, which uses giant machines to scrape away the surface of the Earth to uncover large seams of coal, has destroyed several million acres of U.S. land over the last 70 years. Each year, an area twice the size of the District of Columbia is dug up.

According to one report by the Government Accounting Office (GAO), strip mines such as those in Colorado, Utah, Nevada, and New Mexico cause a change in the soil's chemical and physical makeup. This change eventually makes the soil unsuitable for agricultural use.

Yet coal producers prefer strip-mining to underground mining for a number of reasons, not the least of which is economic. Because strip-mining requires the use of fewer miners, it's far more profitable than underground mining.

Objections to strip-mining based on the irreversible damage it does to the land have been eased somewhat by promises from coal producers to "repair" stripped lands by filling, fertilizing, seeding, and watering the lands following mining operations. Yet the revegetation of many areas, according to a GAO report, "can only be accomplished with good management and major sustained inputs of water and fertilizer. And, in the case of [the] drier areas of the West, even these efforts may not reclaim the land."

In the meantime, strip-mining continues throughout the Southwest. In the process, the big loser is the environment.[5]

THE SOLAR ALTERNATIVE

There is a solution. It involves using alternative energy sources. In Hawaii, which imports over 90 percent of its oil, concerned citizens had installed 45,000 nonpolluting solar systems for heating and hot-water generation as of 1986. In order to help pay for the installations, state lawmakers approved a solar tax program that offered a 15-percent tax break in 1986. The deduction was designed to help replace the loss of a 40-percent federal tax credit that ended in 1985.

By encouraging the installation of solar systems, Hawaii saved more than 315,000 barrels of oil worth $6 million in 1987 alone. That averaged out to nearly 7 barrels per household. The credits cost the state $10 million.

But the 15 percent tax credit wasn't enough to save Hawaii's solar industry, according to Rick Reed of the Hawaii Solar Energy Association. When the federal government phased out its credit system, the number of new solar installations dropped to 1,000 units in 1986—down 700 percent from 1985. Most of the state's top solar firms have since either gone out of business or are tottering on the verge of bankruptcy.[6]

ENCROACHING CIVILIZATION

People, too, are helping to upset the delicate balance of nature in the Southwest. Utah's Glen Canyon was once regarded as the most beautiful, enchanting sandstone canyon on the Colorado River. But no more. It was backfilled with water in 1964 to create Lake Powell—a tragedy in itself but far from the end of the story.

Today, the area faces total destruction. Most of the problem centers around Bullfrog Marina, a growing resort community within the recreational area of Lake Powell's north shore.

Visitors to Bullfrog topped 247,000 in 1987, up from 70,000 just a decade earlier. The jump in numbers was enough to attract corporate builder Del Webb Recreational Properties. Webb has since added motels, restaurants, gas stations, and boat-rental concession stands to the community.

The results have been predictable: increased water pollution, poorer air quality, and a shrinking natural habitat. As if that weren't bad enough, local officials hope to build an airport on the opposite shore of the lake to attract even more tourists. These, they hope, will deposit even more dollars in Bullfrog's economy before they depart.

Environmentalists concerned with the area's deterioration have petitioned for an Environmental Impact Statement and review by the Environmental Protection Agency (EPA) in the hope that the area may prove unsuitable for an airport. Meanwhile, as more and more people move out of existing metropolitan areas and into Bullfrog, they clear land for houses, dig wells for fresh water, and lay septic systems for waste disposal. They also carve roads and driveways through undeveloped areas and generate garbage and other wastes that must be disposed of safely, a problem of immense proportion.

CAUTION
TOXIC SUBSTANCES

OUR THROWAWAY SOCIETY

America today is literally burying itself beneath tons of garbage. In the 1920s, each U.S. citizen threw away an average of 2.75 pounds of solid wastes a day. By 1985, that figure had risen to 4 pounds a day. And that's only household trash, not agricultural, mining, and industrial wastes.[7]

In the 1950s, the problem seemed to have been solved as engineers developed a plan for landfilling trash and covering each day's waste with a layer of soil. The result was called a sanitary landfill. Although anything but sanitary, the landfills nonetheless produced fewer foul smells and rats than earlier open landfills and dumps.

But recent studies show that many landfills are leaching toxic chemicals into groundwater tables. To make matters worse, many communities in the Southwest are running out of places to put their trash. Most landfills today are operating near or beyond capacity, and places where people will allow new landfills to be constructed are increasingly difficult to find.[8] As a result, a new industry sprang up in the 1980s. The illegal dumping of toxic wastes generated by chemical and manufacturing plants in such cities as Los Angeles, Denver, and Albuquerque resulted in spiraling pollution levels throughout the Southwest. Since then, the problem has gotten worse.

The EPA estimates that up to 90 percent of all toxic waste is currently dumped illegally or unsafely. So much money is involved in these so-called "midnight dumpings" that organized crime has gotten involved, according to author David Day in his book, *The Environmental Wars*. "There are tens of thousands of illegal dumps, many of which will result in leakages and poisonings at least as bad as that at Love Canal [in New York]," writes Day. "Large criminal organizations are deeply involved in this illegal business, and it is kept going by considerable political corruption.

"Law enforcement officials and environmental agencies have an uphill struggle enforcing regulations, or even investigating sites in such an atmosphere."

Still, some progress is being made. In Los Angeles in 1984, investigations by a specially created Toxic Waste Strike Force resulted in the imprisonment of 12 high-ranking company offi-

Toxic Substances Discharged by U.S. Industry, 1987

Destination	Millions of Pounds
Air	2700
Lakes, Rivers and Streams	550
Landfills and Earthen Pits	3900
Treatment and Disposal Facilities	3300
Total	10450

Source: Environmental Protection Agency, reported in *The Washington Post*, April 13, 1989, p. A33

(opposite page)
Toxic waste remains one of the Southwest's most serious environmental problems.

cials for the illegal dumping of hazardous waste. The Los Angeles district attorney has since sent a clear message to both industrial and criminal polluters: "Hazardous waste dumping is a violent crime against the community" that would not be tolerated in his city.[9]

RECYCLING

One of the most promising means of reducing the amount of waste—both toxic and otherwise—is called recycling, the removal from the waste pile of those items that may have market value as new and useful materials. Discarded rubber tires, for instance, may be turned into pavement for new roads. Today's discarded newspaper may be turned into tomorrow's books, pamphlets, and notepads.

The most efficient way to separate recyclable materials from nonrecyclable materials is at their source: the homes, businesses, and factories that generate the trash.

During the month of December 1982, nearly 640 tons of newspaper, 150 tons of glass, 20 tons of aluminum cans, and 36 tons of steel were collected for recycling in the community of Marin County, California, just north of San Francisco. Similar voluntary recycling programs are in effect in cities throughout the Southwest, and legislators are currently considering making the recycling of certain materials mandatory by the year 1995.

Once our mountains of waste are too large to control, it will be too late. Runoff from rainwater will continue leaching toxic chemicals from landfills into our streams, rivers, lakes, ponds, and even our underground water supplies. When the water is gone, what will we drink?

NUCLEAR WASTE

Another even more frightening form of pollution concerns radioactive waste from nuclear power plants.

The same principles that govern the making of a nuclear bomb apply to making a nuclear reactor for the generation of electricity. When the nucleus from an atom is split, the neutrons released in the process bombard other atoms, splitting

them and releasing additional neutrons, which in turn bombard still more atoms. Each time an atom splits, it generates heat. The amount of energy produced can be adjusted by controlling the number of atoms split.

Recycling glass bottles can help reduce landfill waste while protecting the environment.

To prevent the process from going too far, nuclear fuel rods containing uranium-235, a radioactive material, are carefully spaced. This allows escaping neutrons to hit enough of the material to start a chain reaction—a self-sustaining bombardment of neutrons—but not enough to result in an explosion.

For every 1,000 grams of uranium-235 fuel that undergoes atomic fission, 999 grams of radioactive waste products are left behind. These are a mixture of solids, liquids, and gases. These waste products must be stored until their radioactivity is no longer harmful to living beings—in some estimates, for more than half a million years!

The United States is temporarily storing about 90 million gallons of radioactive wastes in underground tanks at nuclear power plants around the country. Some of these wastes have been in storage for more than 20 years—sometimes in unlabeled containers. Investigators recently discovered several radioactive drums buried in a landfill in Beatty, Nevada. The drums were leaking radioactive material into the ground.

Something must be done with the nuclear waste already on hand, as well as with that still to be created. The U.S. Department of Energy (DOE) is currently in the process of selecting a permanent storage site in the Southwest. It is this area of the country that DOE considers to be most stable and thus best suited to storing radioactive wastes. The department proposes packing these wastes in metal and concrete containers and storing them deep underground in geologic formations that have been stable for millions of years—either in salt, granite, basalt, or volcanic rock formations.

DOE thought it had located the perfect site for dumping the nation's low-level radioactive waste—waste with a life span of a few hundred years—in underground salt caves in New Mexico, just 26 miles from Carlsbad Caverns. But as the world's first permanent Waste Isolation Pilot Plant (WIPP) neared completion, people began having doubts.

In September 1988, several DOE engineers issued a report questioning the safety of the $680 million facility. This forced the department to postpone indefinitely WIPP's scheduled October opening. Among the engineers' concerns was the fear that moisture and salt in the caverns could combine to form a corrosive substance strong enough to eat through the steel storage drums. This could release radioactive materials into the Pecos River. Thousands of miles of terrain and countless plant and animal species could be destroyed.

Another serious concern involves transporting the waste to its proposed storage facility. Storage containers have repeatedly failed to pass impact tests. In addition, very little money has been put aside to train and equip emergency-response teams along proposed shipping routes crossing more than 20 states. To make matters worse, DOE has repeatedly come under fire for lax management and unsafe handling of nuclear wastes at nearly all of its 17 nuclear weapons facilities.

Meanwhile, low-level radioactive waste from 45 years of atomic-weapons production continues to mount at plants across the nation. Most of this "hot" trash consists of gloves, clothing, tools, and equipment contaminated with plutonium and other radioactive isotopes. It also includes toxic solvents, heavy metals, and decomposing organic matter. As long ago as 1969, low-level nuclear waste proved a major problem when a nuclear dump site in Colorado spontaneously ignited, scattering plutonium dust over a wide area. Since then, the amount of radioactive waste has more than doubled.

To date, DOE has invested nearly $700 million in WIPP. The agency desperately needs a national repository for nuclear wastes if it's to carry out plans to update and clean up its nuclear weapons plants.

At least one member of Congress is skeptical. "We have waste we aren't sure about, [stored] in containers that haven't been approved, traveling over roads that haven't been improved, being put in salt beds that we don't know about," says New Mexico senator Tom Rutherford. "We'd like to put the brakes on before we get to the edge of the cliff."

Besides continuing its support for WIPP, DOE has plans for entombing high-level refuse—radioactive sludge and spent fuel rods from nuclear reactors—in a similar site beneath Nevada's Yucca Mountain.

POWER PLANTS SHUT DOWN

But while DOE continues its search for nuclear-waste storage facilities, some citizens have decided that even a little nuclear waste is too much. In June 1989, voters in Sacramento, California, shut down the Rancho Seco nuclear power plant despite a $580,000 campaign by the nuclear industry to keep the plant open.[10] The Sacramento vote has since influenced decisions to shut down several other reactors, including one at Fort St. Vrain, Colorado. The Public Service Company of Colorado (PSC) closed the plant down in 1989 after nearly 10 years of problems. Current plans call for PSC and several other companies to spend $350 million to "decommission" the plant, store its spent nuclear fuel, and convert Fort St. Vrain into a conventional gas-fired power company.

Where is the nuclear industry headed in the Southwest? Will nuclear energy be able to provide clean, safe fuel for the future, as supporters insist? Can nuclear energy and the ecosystem coexist? These are questions no one can answer yet. But they must be addressed before a major tragedy occurs.

THE AIR WE BREATHE

If the Earth is the heart of the great American Southwest, the skies are its lungs. Besides providing oxygen and other gases for plants and animals living on Earth, the atmosphere acts as a shield. It protects the Earth from harmful radiation coming from the sun and distant stars. Without this protection, Earth's surface temperatures would soar, and every living thing would soon burn to a crisp.

Although the makeup of the atmosphere has remained relatively unchanged for millions of years, something has happened in the last century that has scientists alarmed. It's called air pollution—the introduction of harmful substances into the atmosphere. One of the most serious aspects of the problem is called the greenhouse effect.

THE GREENHOUSE EFFECT

Carbon dioxide absorbs and holds heat from the sun as it reflects off the Earth's surface. The amount of gas in the atmosphere is increased by burning fossil fuels such as coal and gasoline. As carbon dioxide increases, Earth's atmosphere retains more and more heat. In time, this excess heat could create an increase in the planet's overall average temperatures of from 2 to 8°F, according to scientists.[1]

An increase of only 3 to 4° could change the world's climate enough to reduce rainfall, trigger worldwide droughts, and result in global famine. Reduced rainfall in the dry Southwest would spell disaster for both plants and animals.

An increase of 5 to 7° could raise the global sea level nearly 2 feet. This could result in large-scale flooding and a serious

(opposite page)
Although the skies over the Southwest look clean and pure, they're actually fouled with numerous toxic chemicals.

loss of valuable crop and recreational lands, especially along the California coast. In addition, rising temperatures could flood large areas of coastal habitat.[2]

Although the concentration of carbon dioxide in the atmosphere has risen only about 14 percent since 1850, the rate at which it's increasing is accelerating yearly. If carbon dioxide continues to build up in the environment, we may have to limit the amount of coal we can use as a fuel during the coming century.

ALL SMOGGED IN

Another common atmospheric problem in and around major cities throughout the Southwest is smog—airborne pollutants from industrial stacks and automobile engine emissions.

Using a specially constructed fumigation chamber at the University of California in Riverside, horticulturist O. Clifton Taylor tests the effects of smog and similar air pollutants on plant life. Taylor's experiments have proved that exhaust gases from automobiles and industrial stacks can slow plant growth, make leaves wither, and cause serious damage to fruit and vegetable crops.

Smog affects everything from houseplants to forests. The exhaust gases from automobiles, a major contributor to smog, have damaged over a million ponderosa pines in the San Bernardino National Forest, 80 miles east of Los Angeles. Statewide, crop losses due to smog pollution topped $30 million in 1980.

Someday soon, Dr. Taylor hopes to find species and strains of plant life that can resist smog. Until then, some residents of the Southwest are looking for other solutions to smog.

On March 17, 1989, the South Coast Association of Governments (SCAG) and the South Coast Air Quality Management District (SCAQMD), representing southern California, voted overwhelmingly to enact a far-reaching plan to make the region's air clean enough to meet federal standards by the early 2000s.

The ambitious three-phase plan requires all cars to be converted to electric power or other clean-burning fuels by 2007. Other aspects of the plan include increased ride sharing; build-

U.S. Sources of Carbon Dioxide Emissions

Electric Utilities	33%
Transportation	31%
Industry	24%
Buildings	12%

Source: MacKenzie, *Breathing Easier* p.10

ing housing nearer to job centers; and placing new controls on electric utilities, oil refineries, industries, and small businesses. Residents will be prohibited from using power lawn mowers and liquid starter fluid for barbecues.

Ozone is one of the principal forms of pollution in an urban society.

   This plan is being hailed by the American Lung Association, the Clean Air Coalition, and other environmental groups. It promises to be the forerunner of similar air-quality plans throughout the country. And that promises good news for the environment.

THE WATER WE DRINK

Water is the common denominator for life on Earth. All life initially evolved from it, and nothing can live without it.

Yet each day, the Southwest, with its low annual rainfall and overall scarcity of water, is exposed to countless sources of water pollution. Lakes that have lived for thousands of years are being threatened by chemical runoff and pollutants from motorboats and nearby housing developments. Rivers and streams are being turned into cesspools as raw sewage and industrial wastes are piped into them. Even the Pacific Ocean—the largest of the world's seas—is staggering beneath the pressures humankind has placed on it.

MINING POLLUTANTS

One major source of water pollution is strip-mining. As coal and other minerals are removed from the mine, the scarred Earth is left behind to generate pollutants. Strip mines expose the iron sulfides in coal to air and water. These sulfides combine with oxygen to form sulfates and sulfuric acid. Water running through strip mines carries these acidic compounds into both underground and surface water systems, where they poison aquatic organisms and damage the ecosystem.

Government estimates show that nearly 7,000 miles of U.S. streams are currently severely contaminated from discharges of acidic water from coal mines. The U.S. Department of the Interior estimates that it would cost between $7 billion and $12 billion to clean up these waterways and an equal amount of money to revegetate old strip-mine sites and return them to their natural state.

(opposite page)
Pure water is rapidly becoming contaminated by acid rain and other airborne pollutants.

Yet despite environmental concerns, strip-mining is on the increase in the southwestern states of Colorado, Nevada, Utah, and New Mexico. It's a cheaper and safer process than underground coal mining, and large coal deposits just below the surface of the Earth lend themselves to quick, easy stripping. Although some regulations governing the operation of strip mines have been enacted on local and state levels, not enough concern has been given to the protection of our waterways.

CHEMICAL POLLUTANTS

Another serious source of water pollution is chemical toxicity—chemical pesticides that remain toxic, or poisonous, long after they're applied. In Clear Lake, California, vacationers bothered by large swarms of annoying gnats treated the lake in 1949, 1954, and 1957 with an insecticide called DDD, a close relative of the powerful pesticide DDT. The DDD was not supposed to harm fish or animals, but eventually the western grebes that feed on fish from the lake began to die off.

Analysis of the birds' fatty tissues showed amounts of DDD up to 1,600 parts per million. Since the poison had been applied at a rate of only 1/50 part per million, scientists were puzzled as to how the deadly pesticide had built up to such levels in the grebes. Additional studies provided the clue. Lake plankton had accumulated 250 times the applied concentration of DDD; frogs, 2,000 times; sunfish, 12,000 times; and grebes, up to 80,000 times.

Scientists soon discovered that the plankton had absorbed the insecticide from the water. It had been consumed by herbivores, or plant eaters, such as young crayfish and snails. The herbivores had, in turn, been eaten by small carnivores, or meat eaters, such as frogs and toads, which in turn were eaten by larger carnivores, such as trout and bass.

By the time the grebes had joined the food chain, concentrations of the insecticide were thousands of times higher than the original application. Since bone and fat are capable of retaining some of the world's most deadly pollutants—including radionuclide strontium-90, PCBs, DDT, and other chlorinated hydrocarbons—the grebes had soon built up deadly concentrations of DDD in their systems.

AGRICULTURAL POLLUTANTS

Although such toxic pesticides as DDD, DDT, and their variations have been banned from use in the United States for decades, many other pesticides and chemical fertilizers, which are used extensively on farms and ranches throughout the Southwest, have not. When heavy rains drench farmers' fields with water, some of these agricultural chemicals end up in our waterways.

Although not all agricultural chemicals are toxic to wildlife, many promote the growth of algae. The algae form a thick, green mat on the surface of lakes, ponds, bays, and slow-moving streams. When the algae die, they settle to the bottom of the water and produce bacteria that choke off the supply of oxygen to both plants and fish, which eventually die.

This overenrichment of waterways from fertilizers and other chemicals is a process known as eutrophication. It's a serious threat to many of the waterways of the Southwest. One of the region's most seriously affected is Lake Tahoe.

Pesticides are a major source of agricultural pollutants in the Southwest.

Cradled among 10,000-foot peaks in the Sierra Nevada mountains of California and Nevada, Lake Tahoe is surrounded by terrain now heavily scored by roads and ski runs. Casinos and luxury hotels sprout from the southern lake shore. Pollutants from motorboats and housing projects foul the once-pure lake waters. Adding to the problem, agricultural runoff from nearby farms makes its way into the lake.

What's worse, Lake Tahoe's slow drainage pattern means that what goes in has a tendency to stay in for a long time. The growth of algae is spreading unchecked, and periodic killoffs of fish are common. Unless the problem is corrected soon, experts fear the lake may become too polluted to support any life at all.

World Land Area Suitable for Agriculture

No Limitations	11%
Too Wet	10%
Too Shallow	22%
Chemical Problems	23%
Too Dry	28%
Unaccounted	6%

Satellite topographical studies show that, of all the world's land, very little is actually suitable for agricultural use.

Source: Essam, El-Hinnawi and Mansur, Hashmi, *The State of the Environment* (London: Butterworths, 1987), p. 36

INCREASING SALINITY

Another problem directly related to agriculture is salinization—an increase in the amount of salt in soil and water. When water is diverted from rivers, lakes, and streams to irrigate nearby farmlands, salt deep within the soil rises to the surface. There it gradually alters the nature of the topsoil and decreases its fertility. Rains and runoff carry surface salts into our waterways, where they change the salinity, or salt content, of the water and poison fish and other aquatic organisms.

Salinization is already a severe problem in the most arid areas of Pakistan, Egypt, Iraq, India, and Australia. However, it's becoming an increasingly serious problem in the American Southwest, where increased irrigation has led to increased salinity of the Rio Grande and Colorado rivers. Unless strict limits are imposed on irrigation soon, those rivers may eventually become too salty to support aquatic life.

FOSSIL FUEL POLLUTANTS

The energy industry also contributes heavily to water pollution. Oil spilled from ships at sea and leaked from offshore wells has resulted in the deaths of hundreds of thousands of seabirds and other marine life.

In 1990, a ship sprang a leak that sent 400,000 gallons of crude oil washing up onto the shore near Huntington Beach,

California. Smaller in size than the spill of the Exxon *Valdez* off the coast of Alaska, the California spill nonetheless claimed the lives of thousands of animals while doing millions of dollars worth of damage to the area's tourism business.

Offshore oil wells, called rigs, are another source of concern to environmentalists. Periodic breakdowns, oil leaks, and seepage from underwater wells add to the amount of oil polluting our oceans. Although the oil industry has developed plans for virtually leak-proof rigs, their construction and installation is extremely costly. Understandably, the industry probably won't use such rigs unless forced by law to do so.

The costs of obtaining oil from the bottom of the sea may rise due to such added safeguards as leak-proof rigs and double-hulled tankers. But the cost to our environment for not taking such precautions is too great to bear.

DAMMED IF YOU DO

Still another problem facing southwestern waterways goes back nearly a century. In 1902, President Theodore Roosevelt created the Bureau of Reclamation to address the problem of too little water throughout the western states. The bureau's approach to the problem was simple. It would build dams to hold back water on rivers that ran to the sea.

And build dams it did, constructing eight on the Colorado River alone since the 1935 erection of Boulder Dam, the river's first. It also built dams on the Green, Rio Grande, and Pecos rivers, as well as many others. In fact, to date, the bureau has created more than 300 storage reservoirs and 350 diversion dams nationwide, plus thousands of miles of canals and pipelines. All this was done for the purpose of moving water from where nature intended it to where humans wanted it to go. The bureau would even have dammed the Grand Canyon in the 1960s except for massive public opposition!

The Bureau of Reclamation accomplished what it set out to do—increase the amount of water available to municipalities and agriculture. But it also accomplished something hardly anyone had foreseen—the closing of thousands of miles of natural river habitat to fish. In the Southwest, dams have driven such native species as the squawfish, or white salmon (a Colorado

species reaching a length of 6 feet), to the very brink of extinction.[1]

In addition to shutting fish out of their natural habitat, dams create another problem. The reservoirs they create—the large artificial lakes behind the dams—were originally intended to save water. But they actually lose more of it to evaporation by exposing large surface areas to the desert sun. Evaporation from the Colorado River's lakes Mead and Powell, for example, amounts to more than 8 percent of the river's flow. This is enough to provide water to 200 cities the size of Flagstaff, Arizona![2]

Newly proposed dam-building projects in the scenic southwestern Canyonlands region of Utah and Arizona caused conservationists to suggest the concept of a new nature preserve—the wild and scenic river. In 1960, the National Park Service proposed to Congress that some of the last free-flowing rivers in the United States be preserved in their natural state.

Congress responded by authorizing the departments of Agriculture and Interior to study the matter. Out of 650 rivers identified throughout the United States, the Wild Rivers Committee from both departments eventually selected 22 of them for possible preservation. President Lyndon Johnson signed the National Wild and Scenic Rivers Act into law in October 1968.[3] The act was a large step toward recognizing the importance of maintaining clean, natural waterways for the benefit of our environment. But it hasn't stopped all new dam proposals.

In Nevada City, California, the Northwest Power Company plans to build two dams on the South Yuba River. Their purpose is to generate additional electricity for the northeastern corridor of the state. But the only two property owners in the area are opposed to the construction.

Northwest Power says it's moving ahead with its plans anyway. Its ace in the hole—a license issued by the Federal Energy Regulatory Commission (FERC) in 1985—guarantees the company federal approval for the project, complete with the right to force the property owners to surrender their lands. Several state agencies opposed to the project have vowed to take the matter to court.

(opposite page)
Although Arizona's Hoover Dam provides power for tens of thousands of homes, it also creates numerous environmental problems.

41

"This has statewide and national implications," says Roger Hicks of the South Yuba River Citizens League. "If developers can take land. . . .in one place, they can do it elsewhere."

Northwest Power counters with the argument that hydroelectric power is "clean and renewable," just the kind of energy that California will need in the future. But Hicks disagrees, quoting state reports that forecast an excess of electrical power through the end of the century and pointing out the environmental damage that the dams will do. "They say that water is a renewable resource," Hicks says. "But they just aren't making many free-flowing rivers these days."

Meanwhile, 800 miles to the southeast, Colorado's North St. Vrain Creek tumbles majestically down the flanks of Mt. Alice in Rocky Mountain National Park. The canyon is regarded as the wildest left on the Colorado Front Range—the only one without a paved road. The state has designated the stream Wild Trout Waters, meaning it should be able to sustain a healthy population of trout without restocking. The canyon through which the stream flows is an important winter refuge for the park's elk, eagles, bighorn sheep, and the heaviest concentration of mountain lions in the state.

All that would have ended in 1986. That's when the Colorado Water Conservation Board, which holds the water rights to North St. Vrain's flow, agreed to allow the St. Vrain/Left Hand Water Conservancy District and the nearby city of Longmont to build two dams in the canyon.

Conservationists appealed to the city of Longmont, which also holds rights to the stream. They convinced city council members to pass a resolution supporting Wild and Scenic protection for the creek. Faced with a long, costly legal battle, the water district eventually dropped its plans for the dams, and the canyon is once again safe—at least for now. But conservationists know it's only a matter of time before someone else comes along and tries to erect a dam on one of the Southwest's few remaining free-flowing rivers.

GOING UNDERGROUND

Throughout the Southwest, fresh groundwater supplies—water stored within the pores of soil and rock formations—are being poisoned by the leaching of hazardous wastes and agricultural and industrial chemicals into the soil. One fifth of California's major drinking-water wells currently contain pollution levels higher than safety limits set by the state. Many of these pollutants are carcinogenic (cancer-causing) chlorinated solvents.

In 1988, hazardous chemicals were detected in the groundwater of 38 states. Although the greatest contributors to polluted groundwater systems are hazardous-waste dumps, agricultural chemicals are not far behind. Each year, American farmers spray or spread 260,000 tons of pesticides and 42 million tons of fertilizers on their fields.

And the problem is just beginning.

Since water moves so slowly through the ground, many of the chemicals applied to the land two or three decades ago haven't yet reached underlying groundwater tables. Once polluted, groundwater is difficult, if not impossible, to cleanse. One underwater aquifer near Norwich in Great Britain was contaminated with whale oil in 1815. It still contained significant toxic residues when wells were dug in 1950.

In a California referendum in November 1986, voters adopted the "Safe Drinking Water and Toxic Enforcement Act." This act, commonly called Proposition 65, passed despite opposition from Governor George Deukmejian and from industry, which spent $4.5 million in an attempt to stop the act.

Under the newly enacted legislation, it's now illegal for anyone to discharge knowingly any significant amounts of carcinogenic chemicals or substances known to cause birth defects. Citizens have the right to sue companies they suspect of violating the new regulations, and the accused companies will have to defend themselves.

The implications of Proposition 65 are far-reaching. Industry is likely to take more care in building its plants far enough from water sources to avoid violating the law. Polluting landfills may eventually cease operations for the same reason. The results should be a cleaner, safer water supply for all California residents. Better still, several other states, concerned about the quality of their water, are looking carefully at the California proposition.

A TIME FOR ACTION

In 1971, the International Union for Conservation of Nature and Natural Resources listed 297 species of mammals and 359 species of birds as being endangered in the United States.

Countless others are threatened—or likely to become endangered—unless current trends are soon reversed. Some 40 species or varieties of U.S. fish have become extinct since 1900, according to *Fisheries* magazine.

In 1977, the National Wildlife Federation published a list of endangered animals that contained 90 endangered species in the Southwest alone. It included birds such as thick-billed parrots, southern bald eagles, and peregrine falcons; large land mammals such as jaguars, ocelots, Sonoran pronghorns, and Mexican wolves; sea mammals such as gray and sperm whales; and reptiles such as hawksbill and leatherback turtles.

Numerous plants and insects are also on the list. The destruction of these species is one more step toward the destruction of humankind.

Each species represents a unique combination of genetic characteristics, called a gene pool. These characteristics enable different species, which are all valuable to humanity, to adapt to varying environmental conditions.

(opposite page)
Once common throughout the Southwest, the American jaguar is now an endangered species.

OUR VANISHING SPECIES

Every year, 1 million acres of land in the United States are placed into development. Some of the species that once lived there move deeper into the remaining "wilderness." Others, such as turtles, fish, insects, and plants, aren't so lucky. They vanish from the area, often forever.

Other factors also threaten wildlife species. Pesticide use, heavy metals, poisonous gases, oil spills, waste disposal, and other by-products of human activities take a heavy toll.

MAINTAINING THE GENE POOL

Sixty years ago, no one would have cared if a soil-dwelling fungus called penicillium became extinct as a result of the destruction of its habitat. Then, quite by accident, Dr. Alexander Fleming discovered that the fungus produces an antibiotic that kills certain microorganisms. By introducing this natural bacteria-killing chemical into the human body, doctors have used penicillin to save hundreds of thousands of lives over the years.

Such beneficial drugs as streptomycin, terramycin, tetracycline, and many others have been found in various bacteria and species of fungi. Some species of higher plants also produce valuable drugs—morphine (from the poppy plant) and quinine (from the cinchona tree), for example. These chemicals were isolated and identified from living organisms and then mass-produced synthetically. What would the world health situation be today if the organisms from which they were discovered had become extinct before the discoveries had been made? The types and numbers of chemical compounds still to be discovered is enormous. Yet once a species is gone, it's gone forever.

Humankind's food production also relies heavily on maintaining a large gene pool. All our crops and livestock have been domesticated from wild plants and animals. The varieties of wheat and rice that currently play a major role in reducing starvation in the world's developing countries are the direct result of breeding experiments using thousands of varieties of these two species. If some of these varieties had been extinct, we might never have created higher yielding crops.

MEETING OUR FOOD REQUIREMENTS

Currently, only three species of plants—rice, wheat, and corn—supply more than half of all human food requirements. Only about 150 kinds of food plants are used extensively, and only 5,000 have ever been used. As we continue to eliminate entire species of plants, we're losing the potential to develop hundreds or even thousands of new food sources to feed a world population in which one out of every three deaths results from starvation. If preserved and carefully managed, the world's species could be a sustainable source of new foods, pharmaceutical chemicals, natural predators of pests, building materials, fuel, and so on.

No matter how much we may wish otherwise, uncontrolled development and unwise use of our lands don't go hand-in-hand with a healthy natural environment. In order to save Earth's remaining species of plants and animals, we need to preserve the environment in which they live. But conflicts between developers and environmentalists often make wildlife preservation difficult.

EARLY ENVIRONMENTALISTS

Around the turn of the century, a few dedicated environmentalists such as Henry David Thoreau, John Muir, Aldo Leopold, and Robert Marshall advocated the enactment of various laws to protect our wilderness areas. When a group of California militia in pursuit of Indians wandered into a Sierra Nevada (California) valley of extraordinary beauty in 1854, conservationists rallied to preserve the area, which the Indians called Yosemite.

A decade later, President Abraham Lincoln signed a bill granting Yosemite Valley and the Mariposa Grove of giant sequoia trees to the state of California "for public use, resort, and recreation."[1] Yosemite and the land at the headwaters of the Yellowstone River in Montana subsequently became America's first public parks in a bill that stipulated "the preservation, from injury or spoliation, of all timber, mineral deposits, natural curiosities or wonders within said park, and their retention in their natural condition."

But the establishment of the parks didn't stop homesteaders, squatters, poachers, commercial fishermen, and ranchers from violating their borders. The situation became so bad that the government was forced to call out the cavalry to rescue the parklands. The army continued to administer the parks for

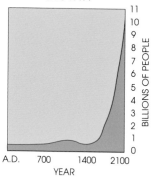

World Population Growth

World population growth and global development are two of the main problems facing the environment.

Sources: Population data from Population Reference Bureau, various publications; historical data from Richard D. Lamm, *Hard Choices* (Denver, CO: May 1985), p. 34

nearly 30 years. Then Congress passed the National Park System Organic Act in 1916, establishing the Park Service that oversees the parks to this day.[2]

During the Great Depression of the 1930s, President Franklin D. Roosevelt helped pass the Civilian Conservation Corps (CCC) act. Employing more than 2.5 million persons during its existence, the CCC act led to the planting of more than 2 million acres of trees and the construction of nearly half a million miles of fire trails, breaks, and forest roads. The nation's national parks and forests were placed under the care of the CCC, which soon established programs to control soil and water erosion and developed recreational facilities, hiking trails, and public roads.

MODERN ENVIRONMENTALISTS

In 1962, Rachel Carson published a book called *Silent Spring* which focused attention on various matters of ecological concern. People suddenly began examining large-scale land developments, agricultural use of pesticides, and industrial sources of air and water pollution in terms of their overall effect on the environment. As a result, more governmental action on antipollution measures ranging from local funding to vast federal projects occurred than ever before in resource-management history.

During the sixties, the U.S. Congress enacted such legislation as the Land and Water Conservation Fund, the Wilderness Act, the Water Resources Research Act, the Open Space Program, and the Clean Air Act. All were aimed at protecting the environment from carelessness, callousness, and greed.

In 1970, in an effort to enforce badly needed environmental laws, Congress established the Environmental Protection Agency (EPA). The EPA soon began conducting studies, making recommendations to Congress, and enforcing new environmental protection laws.

Although the EPA was an organization whose time had clearly come, its powers were inadequate to produce the desired results. Political infighting and selfish regional interests prevented the agency from acting on the great majority of problems it identified as needing immediate attention.

THE CLEAN WATER ACT

In 1972, Congress passed the Clean Water Act, making wetlands protection and water-pollution control part of the EPA's responsibility. But as conservation budgets declined, many of the most effective wetland controls have come from privately funded conservation organizations such as the Nature Conservancy, the Audubon Society, and Ducks Unlimited. These and other groups have purchased large tracts of private land for conservation purposes.

Recently, the federal government has again assumed a more active role in the protection of our environment. In a renewed effort to flex its environmental muscles, Congress in 1985 passed the Food Security Act. This act denies federal aid such as price-support payments, crop insurance, and low-interest loans to farmers who convert wetlands or highly erodible lands to croplands. With these and similar laws to spur action, many environmentalists feel the time for change is now.

In their book, *The House We Live In*, authors Blau and Rodenbeck say, "We have learned that we are not merely in danger of being blown up; we are also in danger of being poisoned by the food we eat, gassed or suffocated by the air we breathe, burned to death by the radiation created for the purpose of peace, or drowned in a sea of our own accumulated filth."

HOPE FOR THE FUTURE

Gradually, a growing sense of awareness by the public is resulting in the realization that our actions in society are never without consequences. Increasing emphasis is being placed on the study and review of new uses of our land, air, and water before those uses take place. In the process, America's natural environment—an environment suffering from severe abuse—faces the best chance of being healed.

But the healing process never comes quickly. It comes instead one step at a time with careful diagnoses and patient, persistent treatment. Hopefully, it's not too late to save the planet—and ourselves—from destruction.

WHAT WE CAN DO

Studies by the Natural Resource Defense Council show that 65 to 70 percent of all U.S. energy is wasted. Yet, more than any other nation on Earth, the United States is a throwaway society. Many people see nothing wrong with drinking from disposable cups, shaving with disposable razors, and carrying groceries home in plastic bags. That doesn't mean they're bad; they're simply uninformed.

With America's output of garbage topping 500,000 tons (1 billion pounds!) a day, the time to begin reducing our mass of trash and keeping other forms of pollution out of the Southwest's fragile environment is now. Everyone can do something to help conserve both energy and natural resources. Here are a few suggestions:

(opposite page)
Recycling is one of the simplest and most effective means of reducing pollution.

FOR THE LAND

- Contact a local group concerned with solid-waste management issues and learn what they're doing to help your community.

- Help organize a field trip with your classmates to a waste-disposal facility.

- Ask your local or school librarian to prepare a presentation or display on the topic of solid-waste disposal.

- Organize a used paper collection system in your school, possibly in the library or media center. Recycling paper saves trees.

- Volunteer to write a story on waste and recycling for your school newspaper.

- Write your mayor and local council members to support the appointment of a full-time recycling coordinator in your community.

- If you live in an area where there are mines, quarries, and mineral reprocessing plants, help organize a school field trip. Find out what these facilities are doing to limit pollution.

- Use cloth instead of paper towels and napkins.

- Buy products that are recyclable, reliable, repairable, refillable, reusable, and in all ways nondisposable.

- Buy beverages in returnable glass containers.

- Stop using hazardous chemicals in your home. Instead of ammonia-based cleansers, use a mixture of vinegar, salt, and water for surface cleaning. For the bathroom, use baking soda and water. For an effective wood polish, use a mixture of one part lemon juice to two parts olive or vegetable oil.

FOR THE AIR

- Learn as much as you can about the major sources of air pollution in your community. Are they motor vehicles, power plants, industrial operations?

- Talk to local park system naturalists to find out if lakes in your area are affected by acid rain. If so, try to learn from what sources the acid rain comes.

- If you live in a rural area that is rarely affected by smog, try to arrange a trip to a major metropolitan area where smog is a serious problem. Afterward, find out what the major cities in your state are doing to limit air pollution.

- Get involved with a local group concerned with the issues of air pollution and support its efforts.

- Eliminate or reduce your own use of air-polluting products, including those containing harmful chlorofluorocarbons (CFCs).

- Suggest that your family drive less and rely more on walking, bicycling, and use of public transportation.

- Plant as many trees around your town as possible. Besides shading buildings in summer, they absorb carbon dioxide and act as natural air filters.

FOR THE WATER

- If you live or vacation near the coast, join an organization concerned with protecting the coastal environment.

- Take up water sports such as swimming, surfing, snorkeling, and diving to give you a greater appreciation for the need for clean water.

- Avoid using products at home that could be damaging to water resources—things such as phosphates in detergents and hazardous household chemicals such as pesticides, acids, paint thinners, etc.

- Make sure your family understands the importance of disposing of waste oil and antifreeze properly—at a gas station or other location with a suitable recycling program.

- Subscribe to newsletters and other publications concerned with the issue of maintaining fresh water quality.

- Ask your local or school librarian to help you prepare a presentation or display on the importance of preventing fresh-water pollution.

- Have your home's hot-water heater insulated and turn its thermostat down to 120° to conserve energy.

- Install sink-faucet aerators and water-saving shower heads to reduce water usage up to 80 percent without decreasing performance.

- Take showers instead of baths and limit them to five minutes.

We no longer live on the same planet our ancestors inhabited. For us, it's an alien planet, one that, in many ways, is hostile, dangerous, and even deadly. We can no longer afford to ignore that fact but must take positive steps to change it.

Only by becoming aware, by being informed, and by taking action toward changing the condition of our planet can we hope for a brighter future—both for ourselves and for future generations.

FOR MORE INFORMATION

The following toll-free hot-line telephone numbers provide information ranging from pesticide use to asbestos in homes; from hazardous-waste disposal to chemical-emergency preparedness.

- Asbestos Hotline (1-800-334-8571). Provides information on asbestos and asbestos abatement programs; Mon. to Fri., 8:15 a.m. to 5 p.m.

- Chemical Emergency Preparedness Program Hotline (1-800-535-0202). For information on community preparedness for chemical accidents, etc.; Mon. to Fri., 8:30 a.m. to 4:30 p.m.

- Inspector General's Whistle Blower Hotline (1-800-424-4000). For confidential reporting of EPA-related waste, fraud, abuse, or mismanagement; Mon. to Fri., 10 a.m. to 3 p.m.

- National Pesticides Telecommunications Network Hotline (1-800-858-7378). Provides information about pesticides, toxicity, management, health and environmental effects, safety practices, and cleanup and disposal; 7 days, 24 hours a day.

- National Response Center Hotline (1-800-424-8802). For reporting oil and hazardous chemical spills; 7 days, 24 hours a day.

- Superfund Hotline (1-800-424-9346). Provides Superfund information and technical assistance; Mon. to Fri., 8:30 a.m. to 4:30 p.m.

(opposite page)
The delicate columbine, Colorado's state flower, may soon become threatened by overdevelopment and pollution.

The following list includes organizations that can provide information and materials on various topics of environmental concern in the Southwest.

American Rivers
Conservation Council
801 Pennsylvania Ave.
SE
Washington, D.C. 20003
202-547-6900

American Water
Resources Association
5410 Grosvenor Lane
Bethesda, MD 20814
301-492-8600

Bio Integral Resource
Center
P.O. Box 8267
Berkeley, CA 94707
415-524-2567

California Coastal
Commission
Federal Programs
Manager
631 Howard St.
San Francisco, CA 94105
415-543-8555

Center for Marine
Conservation
1725 DeSales St. NW
Washington, D.C. 20036
202-429-5609

Citizen's Clearinghouse
for Hazardous Wastes
P.O. Box 926
Arlington, VA 22216
703-276-7070

Citizens for Ocean Law
1601 Connecticut Ave.
NW
Washington, D.C. 20009
202-462-3737

Consumer Product
Safety Commission
Western Regional Office
555 Battery St.
Room 415
San Francisco, CA 94111
415-705-1816

Council for Solid Waste
Solutions
1275 K St. NW
Washington, D.C. 20005
202-371-5319

Earth First!
Box 5871
Tucson, AZ 85703
607-622-1371

Environmental Action
1525 New Hampshire
Ave. NW
Washington, D.C. 20036
202-745-4870

Environmental Defense
Fund
1616 P St. NW
Washington, D.C. 20036
202-387-3500

Friends of the Earth
218 D St. SE
Washington, D.C. 20003
202-544-2600

Greenpeace USA
1436 U St. NW
Washington, D.C. 20009
202-462-1177

National Association for
Plastic Container
Recovery
5024 Parkway Plaza
Blvd.
Charlotte, NC 28217
704-357-3250

National Audubon
Society
950 Third Ave.
New York, NY 10022
212-546-9100

National Clean Air
Coalition
801 Pennsylvania Ave.
SE
Washington, D.C. 20003
202-543-8200

National Geographic
Society
17th and M Streets NW
Washington, D.C. 20036
202-857-7000

National Wildlife
Federation
1400 16th St. NW
Washington, D.C. 20036
202-637-3700

The Nature Conservancy
1815 N. Lynn St.
Arlington, VA 22209
703-841-4860

Rocky Mountain
Institute
1739 Snowmass Creek
Road
Drawer 248
Old Snowmass, CO
81654
303-927-3851

Save San Francisco Bay
Association
P.O. Box 925
Berkeley, CA 94701
415-849-3044

Sea Shepherd
Conservation Society
P.O. Box 7000
South Redondo Beach,
CA 90277
213-373-6979

Sierra Club
530 Bush St.
San Francisco, CA 94108
415-981-8634

Southwest Research and
Information Center
P.O. Box 4524
Albuquerque, NM 87106
505-262-1862

Treepeople
12601 Mulholland Dr.
Beverly Hills, CA 90210
213-273-8733

The Trust for Public
Land
116 New Montgomery
St., 4th Floor
San Francisco, CA 94105
415-495-4014

United Nations
 Environment Program
1889 F St. NW
Washington, D.C. 20006
202-289-8456

U.S. Dept. of Agriculture
Independence Ave.
 between 12th and 14th
 Streets SW
Washington, D.C. 20250
202-477-8732

U.S. Environmental
 Protection Agency
401 M St. SW
Washington, D.C. 20460
202-382-2090

U.S. Fish and Wildlife
 Service
Dept. of the Interior
Washington, D.C. 20240
202-343-7445

CHAPTER TWO: THE LAND WE WALK

1. David Rains Wallace, *Life in the Balance* (New York: Harcourt Brace Jovanovich, Publishers, 1987), p. 136.
2. Ibid, pp. 123 - 125.
3. Richard H. Wagner, *Environment and Man* (New York: W. W. Norton & Company, 1974), pp. 39 - 40.
4. *The Global Ecology Handbook* (Boston: Beacon Press, 1990), p. 77.
5. Wagner, *Environment and Man*, pp. 26 - 28.
6. Rich Budnick, "Solar Takes a Nosedive," *Environmental Action*, September/October 1987, p. 7.
7. *The Global Ecology Handbook*, p. 267.
8. Ibid, p. 276.
9. David Day, *The Environmental Wars* (New York: St. Martin's Press, 1989), pp. 213 - 214.
10. Jon Naar, *Design for a Livable Planet* (New York: Harper & Row, 1990), p. 168.

CHAPTER THREE: THE AIR WE BREATHE

1. *The Global Ecology Handbook*, pp. 231 - 232.
2. *The Universal Almanac 1990* (Kansas City, MO: Universal Press Syndicate Company, 1989), pp. 370 - 371.

CHAPTER FOUR: THE WATER WE DRINK

1. Wallace, *Life in the Balance*, pp. 186 - 187.
2. Ibid, p. 187.
3. Ibid, p. 191.

CHAPTER FIVE: A TIME FOR ACTION

1. Wallace, *Life in the Balance*, p. 104.
2. Ibid, p. 105.

G L O S S A R Y

Acid rain. Rain containing a high concentration of acids from various pollutants such as sulfur dioxide, nitrogen oxide, etc.

Air pollution. The transfer of contaminating substances into the atmosphere, usually as a result of human activities.

Algae. Primitive green plants, many of which are microscopic.

Aquatic. Of or relating to life in the water.

Aquifer. Water-bearing rock or soil.

Atmosphere. A mass of gases surrounding the Earth.

Biological control. The use of a pest's natural predators and parasites to control its population.

Biome. A specific environment capable of supporting life.

Biosphere. That part of the Earth, including its atmosphere, capable of supporting life.

Carcinogen. A substance known to cause cancer.

Desertification. The usually gradual changeover of arable land into desertlike wasteland.

Drought. A prolonged period without precipitation.

Dust. Tiny particulate materials that are primarily the product of wind erosion of soil.

Ecology. The branch of science concerned with the interrelationship of organisms and their environment.

Ecosystem. A functioning unit of the environment that includes all living organisms and physical features within a given area.

Erosion. The removal and transportation of soil by wind, running water, or glaciation.

Eutrophication. A natural process in which lakes gradually become too productive, often due to the introduction of growth-stimulating materials such as phosphates.

Extinction. The disappearance of an organism from Earth.

Fertilizer. A substance used to make soil more productive.

Food chain. A sequence of organisms in which each member feeds on the member below it, such as an owl, rabbit, and grass.

Fossil fuels. Various fuel materials such as coal, oil, and natural gas created from the remains of once-living organisms.

Fungus. Primitive plants such as mushrooms, blights, and rusts.

Gene pool. The total characteristics possessed by a particular species.

Greenhouse effect. The increase in solar-radiated infrared light waves in Earth's atmosphere; the increase is caused by an accumulation of such gases as methane, nitrogen oxides, ozone, and chlorofluorocarbons (CFCs).

Groundwater. Water that is contained in subsurface rock and soil formations.

Hazardous waste. The extremely dangerous by-product of civilization that, by its chemical makeup, is harmful to life.

Humus. The organic portion of soil consisting mostly of partially decomposed plant or animal matter.

Irrigation. The process of diverting water from its source to farmland in order to increase crop yields.

Landfill. A site for the disposal of garbage and other waste products.

Leaching. The dissolving and transporting of materials by water seeping downward through soil.

Mineral. A solid material characterized by an orderly internal arrangement of atoms and a fixed chemical composition.

Nuclear energy. Energy from the nucleus of an atom.

Nuclear waste. The long-lived, extremely dangerous by-product of nuclear energy or nuclear weapons production.

Ozone. A gas naturally present in the atmosphere; also, an artificially produced gas that is a major ingredient in smog.

Pesticide. A general term for any of a large number of chemical compounds used to kill pests such as insects, weeds, fungi, bacteria, etc.

Photosynthesis. The process by which light energy is converted by green plants into chemical energy for food.

Pollution. A general term for environmental contaminants.

Recycling. The recovery and reuse of material resources.

Rock. A stonelike material usually composed of a combination of minerals.

Runoff. Water that moves across the surface of the land faster than the soil can absorb it.

Salinization. The increase of salt in soil or water.

Sanitary landfill. A site consisting of alternate layers of trash and soil.

Sewage. Refuse liquid or waste matter carried by sewers.

Smog. A visible mixture of solid, liquid, and gaseous air pollutants that are harmful both to human beings and to the environment.

Soil. A living system of weathered rock, organic matter, air, and water in which plants grow.

Strip-mining. A method of surface mining that takes in a wide area and is usually used for the removal of coal near the Earth's surface.

Toxic waste. The extremely dangerous by-product of chemical production or use.

Water pollution. The transfer of contaminating substances into water, usually as a result of human activities.

Water table. The highest level of a groundwater reservoir.

Weathering. The chemical decomposition or physical changing of rocks into smaller particles.

Wetlands. Land containing a high moisture content.

BIBLIOGRAPHY

As We Live and Breathe. Washington, D.C.: National Geographic Society, 1971.

Budiansky, Stephen, and Robert F. Black. "Tons and Tons of Trash and No Place To Put It." *U.S. News and World Report*, Dec. 14, 1987, pp. 58 - 62.

Budnick, Rich. "Solar Takes a Nosedive." *Environmental Action*, September/October 1987, p. 7.

Caplan, Ruth. *Our Earth, Ourselves*. New York: Bantam Books, 1990.

Day, David. *The Environmental Wars*. New York: St. Martin's Press, 1989.

The Earth Report. Los Angeles: Price Stern Sloan, Inc., 1988.

Grossman, Karl. *The Poison Conspiracy*. Sag Harbor, NY: The Permanent Press, 1983.

Marx, Wesley. "Environmental Countdown." *Reader's Digest*, May 1990, p. 99.

Moran, Joseph M., Michael D. Morgan, and James H. Wiersma. *An Introduction to Environmental Sciences*. Boston: Little, Brown and Company, 1973.

Steinhart, Peter. "Empty the Skies." *Audubon*, November 1987, p. 70.

Stuller, Jay. "Weary Tahoe Combatants Try Compromise." *Audubon*, May 1987, p. 44.

Wagner, Richard H. *Environment and Man*. New York: W. W. Norton & Co., Inc., 1974.

Wallace, David Rains. *Life in the Balance*. New York: Harcourt Brace Jovanovich, 1987.